Drama for Students, Volume 4

Staff

Editorial: David M. Galens, *Editor*. Terry Browne, Christopher Busiel, Clare Cross, John Fiero, David M. Galens, Carole Hamilton, D. L. Kellett, Erika Kreger, Sheri Metzger, Daniel Moran, Terry Nienhuis, Arnold Schmidt, William P. Wiles, Etta Worthington, *Entry Writers*. Elizabeth Cranston, Catherine V. Donaldson, Kathleen J. Edgar, Jennifer Gariepy, Dwayne D. Hayes, Joshua Kondek, Tom Ligotti, Scot Peacock, Patti Tippett, Pam Zuber, *Contributing Editors*. James Draper, *Managing Editor*. Diane Telgen, *"For Students" Line Coordinator*. Jeffery Chapman, *Programmer/Analyst*.

Research: Victoria B. Cariappa, *Research Team Manager*. Andy Malonis, Barb McNeil, *Research Specialists*. Julia C. Daniel, Tamara C. Nott, Tracie A. Richardson, Cheryl L. Warnock, *Research Associates*. Phyllis P. Blackman, Jeffrey D. Daniels,

Corrine A. Stocker, *Research Assistants.*

Permissions: Susan M. Trosky, *Permissions Manager.* Kimberly F. *Smilay Permissions Specialist.* Steve Cusack and Kelly A. Quin, *Permissions Associates.*

Production: Mary Beth Trimper, *Production Director.* Evi Seoud, *Assistant Production Manager.* Shanna Heilveil, *Production Assistant.*

Graphic Services: Randy Bassett, *Image Database Supervisor.* Robert Duncan and Michael Logusz, *Imaging Specialists.* Pamela A. Reed, *Photography Coordinator.* Gary Leach, *Macintosh Artist.*

Product Design: Cynthia Baldwin, *Product Design Manager.* Cover Design: Michelle DiMercurio, *Art Director.* Page Design: Pamela A. E. Galbreath, *Senior Art Director.*

Copyright Notice

editors or publisher. Errors brought to the attention of the publisher and verified to the satisfaction of the publisher will be corrected in future editions.

This publication is a creative work fully protected by all applicable copyright laws, as well as by misappropriation, trade secret, unfair competition, and other applicable laws. The authors and editors of this work have added value to the underlying factual material herein through one or more of the following: unique and original selection, coordination, expression, arrangement, and classification of information. All rights to this publication will be vigorously defended.

This book is printed on acid-free paper that meets the minimum requirements of American National Standard for Information Sciences—Permanence Paper for Printed Library Materials, ANSI Z39.48-1984.

ISBN 0-7876-2753-4
ISSN 1094-9232
Printed in the United States of America

10 9 8 7 6 5 4

Death and the Maiden

Ariel Dorfman 1991

Introduction

Ariel Dorfman's *Death and the Maiden* is a moral thriller about a woman, Paulina, who believes that a stranger who comes to her home is the doctor who, under a military dictatorship, tortured and raped her many years before. (The play's title is taken from a piece of music by Franz Schubert; Paulina loved the piece but grew to revile it when it was played repeatedly during her torture sessions.) Dorfman began writing the play in the mid-1980s, when he was in exile from Chile, a country under the rule of the military dictator General Augusto Pinochet. It was not until Chile's return to democracy in 1990 that Dorfman returned to the play and "understood. . . how the story had to be told." A workshop production of *Death and the Maiden* was staged in Santiago, Chile, opening in March, 1991, and in July of that year the play had its world premiere at London's Royal Court Upstairs. In November the production, which received the London *Time Out* Award for best play of 1991, moved to the Royal Court Mainstage. Reception of the play was positive, critics finding it both dramatically engaging as well as historically timely (given the number of societies around the world facing painful legacies of repressive regimes).

The play had its Broadway premiere on March 17, 1992, directed by Mike Nichols and starring Glenn Close as Paulina (a performance for which she received an Antionette "Tony" Perry Award), Richard Dreyfuss as Gerardo, and Gene Hackman as Miranda. The casting of three Anglo actors in a play with a Latin American context was protested by Latino organizations and the Actors' Equity Association (the union for American actors). Dorfman's play, ultimately, did not receive as high praise in the United States as it had in England but did create enough interest to inspire a film adaptation in 1994. *Death and the Maiden* is valued as a dramatic work that examines the psychological repercussions of human rights abuses.

Author Biography

Playwright, essayist, novelist, poet, and short story writer Ariel Dorfman was born in Buenos Aires, Argentina, on May 6, 1942, the son of an economist and a literature teacher. His life illustrates the fragmented experience of the modern Latin American exile. At the age of two, his family was forced to flee to the United States because of his father's opposition to the Argentine government of Juan Peron. Dorfman's father was one of the architects of the United Nations, and the family lived in New York for ten years before leaving in 1954, during the McCarthy era, to settle in Chile. Completing a University education, Dorfman became a naturalized Chilean citizen in 1967. Working for the next several years as a journalist and activist, he published several works, including a study of the plays of Harold Pinter (*The Homecoming*).

A supporter of Chilean President Salvador Allende, Dorfman was forced into exile after a military coup led by General Augusto Pinochet seized control of the country in 1973. He intermittently lived in Argentina, France, the Netherlands, and eventually settled in the United States (in 1980), holding a variety of academic posts in each of the countries. In 1984 he became a professor at Duke University in Durham, North Carolina, where he maintains a part-time residence. Remaining active in Chile's political and social affairs while in exile, Dorfman first tried to return home to Chile in 1983 yet felt uncomfortable in the environment there. He tried a part-time return in 1986, but the following year, he was stopped at Santiago airport, detained, and then deported. Dorfman returned to Chile again in 1989. Following Pinochet's abdication to a popularly-elected president in 1990, the playwright attempted to re-establish a semi-permanent residence in his adopted homeland.

Dorfman's writings have been translated into over twenty languages. Like many other Latin American authors, he is also a social critic who investigates the relationship between politics and culture. He is the author of important essays and works of cultural criticism—*How to Read Donald Duck: Imperialist Ideology in the Disney Comic* (1975), *Culture and Resistance in Chile* (1978) and *The Empire's Old Clothes* (1980)—which argue that popular literatures promote capitalist and neo-imperial ideology and encourage passivity. Dorfman has additionally written literary works in a variety of forms. His collections of short stories include *The Medicine Goes Down* (1985) and *My House Is on Fire* (1979) which examines how people retain a sense of hope living under an oppressive military regime. Dorfman's novels have been praised for their highly original narrative techniques. *The Last Song of Manuel Sendero* (1987) combines several different perspectives, including those of cartoon characters and the unborn. *Mascara* (1988) explores human identity and the paranoia created by authoritarian regimes.

Dorfman's many collections of poetry include *Missing* (1982) and *Last Waltz in Santiago and Other Poems of Exile and Disappearance* (1986). In the theater—besides his success with *Death and the Maiden* (1991)—Dorfman has created stage adaptations of his novel *Widows* (1981) and his short story "Reader" (1979).

Act I

When the play opens, "The time is the present and the place, a country that is probably Chile but could be any country that has given itself a democratic government just after a long period of dictatorship." At the Escobar's secluded beach house it is late at night and an uneaten dinner is laid out on the table. Paulina sits on the terrace, startled by the sound of an unfamiliar car motor. She takes a gun from the sideboard, and stands listening as her husband, Gerardo, speaks to the driver of the car and then enters the house. Paulina is disturbed by the unusual occurrence, and Gerardo explains that he had a flat tire on the way home and accepted a ride from a passing motorist. He blames Paulina for the spare tire being flat and for the jack being gone (Paulina lent it to her mother). The couple argue about these details and then discuss Gerardo's meeting with the country's president, from which he has just returned.

Gerardo has been named to a commission examining human rights abuses under the country's previous government, a military dictatorship. (It is revealed through dialogue that Paulina was arrested and tortured while attending medical school during this dictatorship.) Paulina has mixed feelings; she is suspicious of the commission, which is only to investigate cases of abuse that ended in death. A case like Paulina's own abduction, therefore, would not fall within the commission's jurisdiction. Paulina is still traumatized by the memory of being raped and tortured, but she has never discussed details of her experience with her mother or other people close to her.

Gerardo agrees with Paulina that the power of the commission is limited, but he believes nevertheless that "there is so much we can do. . . ." Gerardo makes a point of appearing to ask for Paulina's permission to sit on the commission, but the first scene ends with his admission that he has already accepted the president's appointment. An hour later, a knock at the door rouses the Escobars. Gerardo is ill at ease until he opens the door to admit Doctor Roberto Miranda, the man who earlier drove him home. Miranda apologizes for the intrusion, and as the two men speak, Paulina edges closer, listening in on their conversation. As she listens, the sound of Miranda's voice appears to greatly upset her. Miranda explains that he heard a news story about the commission on the radio, only then realizing who Gerardo was, and felt he had to return to congratulate him on the appointment. Miranda appears very enthusiastic about the commission, although he also realizes that the investigations are unlikely to conclude with punishment. Miranda prepares to leave, promising to pick Gerardo up the next morning and help him retrieve his car, but Gerardo insists that Miranda stay the night.

The third scene is a brief interlude a short time later, in which Paulina is seen dragging Miranda's unconscious body into the room and tying him to a chair. She gags him with her own underwear, then takes his car keys and leaves. When dawn rises on the fourth scene, Paulina has returned and sits with her gun, watching Miranda. When he awakens, she speaks to him for a long while, playing a cassette of Schubert's quartet *Death and the Maiden* which she found in Miranda's car. This music has painful associations for Paulina; it was played while she was in captivity, and Paulina takes Miranda's cassette—along with the familiarity of his voice—as proof that he is the doctor who tortured her. Gerardo enters, aghast at the scene he finds. Paulina explains her discovery, and Gerardo's first conclusion is: "You're sick." Gerardo makes a move to untie Miranda, and Paulina fires the gun wildly. She explains that she has already called a mechanic, and when the latter arrives, she ushers Gerardo out of the house to retrieve their car. The act ends with Paulina's cool statement, "We're going to put him on trial, Gerardo, this doctor. Right here, today."

Act II

The time is midday; Miranda is still tied and Paulina speaks to him intimately about her captivity and the night of her release. Gerardo enters after retrieving the car, with a new resolve to talk his wife into releasing Miranda. Gerardo appeals to an ideal of law, implying Paulina is no better than the military regime if she will not allow Miranda to defend himself. Paulina says she has every intention of allowing the doctor to argue his case. She was only waiting for Gerardo's return, having decided that her husband will act as a lawyer for the accused. When Paulina removes his gag, Miranda claims never to have seen Paulina before, calling her "extremely ill, almost prototypically schizoid."

Gerardo continues to plead with his wife, and as they argue it becomes evident that Gerardo has difficulty speaking about Paulina's experience. If she can prove beyond a shadow of a doubt that Miranda is the same doctor, Paulina asks, would Gerardo still want her to set him free. Gerardo replies, "If he's guilty, more reason to set him free. . . . Imagine what would happen if everyone acted like you did." Gerardo argues that if Miranda is guilty of the crimes, they should turn him over to the proper authorities. His wife, however, believes that while the new government calls itself a democracy, many of the same men who were part of the dictatorship are still active in the government. Not only does she contend that the authorities would immediately release Miranda, she states her belief that the doctor is part of the current government and that his encounter with Gerardo was no coincidence.

Paulina explains that at one point she wanted retribution from Miranda but says that now she merely wants him to confess and she will let him go. "What can he confess if he's innocent?" wonders Gerardo. The scene ends on Paulina's reply, "If he's innocent? Then he's really screwed."

The second scene is at lunch. Paulina watches from the terrace as Gerardo feeds Miranda and the two men talk. Gerardo stresses that a confession, even a false one, is Miranda's only hope of escaping unharmed, while Miranda emphasizes that he is only in his current situation because he stopped to pick up Gerardo and now depends on the lawyer to get him out of this mess. After another threatening appearance by Paulina, Miranda accuses Gerardo of not being as impartial as he has claimed to be: "She plays the bad guy and you play the good guy. . . to see if you can get me to confess that way." The two men argue but eventually admit they are both scared, and the act ends with Miranda asking Gerardo's help in fabricating a convincing confession for Paulina.

Act III

The final act opens just before evening. Miranda is still bound, and Gerardo, with a tape recorder on his lap, pleads with Paulina to tell him the details of her abduction before he has to hear them from Miranda. Paulina reminds him that she had attempted to tell him these details before, just after she was released, when they were interrupted by the woman with whom Gerardo was involved during Paulina's absence. This memory is a severe blow to Gerardo, and he eventually persuades Paulina to speak instead of her abduction. When she gets to the point in her story of first meeting the doctor and hearing Schubert in the darkness, the lights fade and her voice overlaps with that of Miranda. The lights come up to reveal Miranda making his confession into the tape recorder. He claims that the music was an attempt to alleviate the suffering of the prisoners. He describes how a "brutalization took over my life," and he began to enjoy the torture with a detached curiosity "partly morbid, partly scientific."

The confession over, Paulina sends Gerardo to retrieve Miranda's car. After his departure, however, she changes her tone, saying she was entirely convinced by the doctor's confession and now "could not live in peace with myself and let you live." She informs him that she inserted small errors in her own taped account, which Miranda apparently corrected of his own accord; now Paulina says she will kill him "because you haven't repented at all." On Paulina's unanswered question, "What do we lose by killing one of them?" the action freezes and the lights go down on the scene.

A giant mirror descends in front of the characters, "forcing," as the stage directions state, "the members of the audience to look at themselves." The lights come up on the final scene of the play, in a concert hall several months later. Gerardo and Paulina enter, elegantly dressed, and sit down facing the mirror. When the music ends they rise as if at intermission, and Gerardo speaks to a number of well-wishers who have gathered around him. Paulina observes Miranda entering ("or he could be an illusion," the directions read.) The three characters are seated as the performance recommences, and Schubert's "Death and the Maiden" is heard. Paulina and Miranda lock eyes for a moment, then she looks ahead into the mirror as the music plays.

Media Adaptations

- *Death and the Maiden* was adapted as a film in 1994, directed by Roman Polanski, and starring Sigourney Weaver as Paulina, Ben Kingsley as Miranda, and Stuart Wilson as Gerardo. Novelist Rafael Yglesias (*Fearless*) and Dorfman wrote the screenplay based on the original play.

Characters

Gerardo Escobar

Paulina's husband, he is a lawyer about forty-five years of age. Gerardo has recently been appointed by the president to a commission that will examine human rights abuses during the military dictatorship. Gerardo has a high ideal of justice which he invokes in an attempt to persuade his wife to release Miranda. Paulina is ethically motivated, too, but she stresses repeatedly that corruption in the country's legal system leaves considerable doubt that the military's abuses will be properly rectified. Gerardo maintains his faith in the government's ability to do the best it can do under the circumstances, while Paulina feels pushed to take matters into her own hands. Undoubtedly, her more personal resolve is the product of her abduction and torment, which Gerardo seems to find almost unfathomable on a personal level, despite the nature of his work.

Gerardo has always had great difficulty discussing Paulina's experience, a guilt that is compounded by the fact that when Paulina went to him following her release, she discovered that he had been having an affair in her absence. Gerardo's suggestion that Paulina make a tape recording may be a way of addressing his problem, putting words to something he has not wanted to face.

Doctor Roberto Miranda

A doctor, around fifty years old. Roberto—Doctor Miranda—remains indignant at Paulina's accusations. He repeatedly reminds Gerardo of his place on the human rights commission and that it is his duty in that capacity to command his wife to release Miranda. The doctor denies having had any role in torturing military abductees and offers a confession that he claims to have fabricated in the hopes that Paulina will release him unharmed. Miranda, however, corrects details in the narrative of Paulina's experience which she recorded for Gerardo; this is enough proof for Paulina that her prisoner is the doctor who raped and tortured her. Miranda does not succeed in convincing her to the contrary but without having to make a direct and true confession he does somehow convince Paulina to spare his life with his plea, "Oh Paulina—isn't it time we stopped?"

Miranda is a mysterious character who Dorfman never fully reveals to the audience. While there is considerable evidence presented that seems to incriminate the doctor, the possibility remains that it is merely coincidence that he fits the profile of Paulina's tormentor. His guilt appears to be further cemented by his decision not to report his kidnapping to the authorities, yet his silence may be attributed to a fear that Gerardo may use his position on the commission to discredit Miranda. Dorfman does not offer explanations for any of these situations. Miranda's fate at the play's conclusion is ambiguous: he may be a guilty man tormented by the atrocities he committed during wartime, or he may be an innocent man terrified by the threat of an unbalanced woman.

Paulina Salas

As a young student in the early days of the military dictatorship that ruled her country (the specific location is never given), Paulina worked with Gerardo helping people seek asylum in embassies and smuggling them out of the country. Paulina's activism, and her medical studies, were cut short, however, when she was arrested by the government. She was tortured and raped repeatedly before finally being released. This devastating experience which so altered her life continues to affect her seventeen years later, when the action of the play occurs.

Paulina has suppressed the worst details of her incarceration. Her paranoia has prevented her from sharing this information with Gerardo or her mother —for fear that the knowledge might place them in danger. While her country has replaced the dictatorship with a free, elected government, she suspects that many in power are from the military and only pretending to be democratic and fair-minded. She lives with acute fear, as can be seen from her defensive actions when Roberto Miranda's unfamiliar car first pulls up to the house. Since her ordeal, Paulina has also stifled a great deal of anger, which surfaces with the opportunity to exact revenge on the man she believes was her primary tormentor. Sure of herself after "trying" Miranda, Paulina appears set to kill the doctor but ultimately chooses to be merciful. This action seems to suggest that she ultimately rejects the idea of an eye for an eye. Yet her humane gesture comes at a price to her piece of mind. The tense final image of the play suggests that Paulina may never be able to achieve a satisfying resolution to her lingering pain.

Themes

Atonement and Forgiveness

While there exists no acceptable rationale for the violence of the military regime, Paulina implies that she can forgive the individual for being fallible: she promises to release Miranda if he will confess to torturing and raping her. Miranda does not genuinely appear to ask for forgiveness; he does so only in the context of a confession which may be falsified. Paulina, although she ultimately chooses not to kill Miranda, does not forgive him, either. The play suggests that despite the lingering pain of political oppression, there is no concrete act that can atone for past wrongs.

Death and the Maiden

The title of Dorfman's play comes from the quartet by Schubert which Paulina associates with her abduction and torture. She finds a cassette of this music in Miranda's car. The piece, String Quartet No. 14 in D minor (D. 810), takes the name "Death and the Maiden" from a Schubert song that is quoted in it. The theme is common in folk music such as the English song "Death and the Lady," in which a rich lady who has failed to bribe Death into granting her a few more years of life sings of having been betrayed by him. The theme of the song (hence the dramatic context for Schubert's quartet) is reflected in the characters themselves, with the shadowy doctor who raped and tortured Paulina existing as a kind of Death figure in her memory. However, Dorfman's play presents a reversal on the theme—if the audience agrees that Paulina has found the right doctor, that is—for in the present circumstance it is the Maiden (Paulina) who holds the power of life over Death (Miranda).

Doubt and Ambiguity

Paulina does not doubt that Roberto Miranda is the doctor who tortured and raped her years before or that he deserves to be tried and punished for these crimes. She is also convinced that she is the only person who can administer a punishment to fit the crime. One of the related themes of *Death and the Maiden*, however, is the lingering ambiguity which troubles a society attempting to rectify wrongs from a turbulent era in its past. Nagging questions remain: who can be sure the correct people are being tried, and what constitutes just punishment? The play examines the consequences of such justice, provoking questions as to the effects such a process will have not only on the accused but on the accuser.

Freedom

The play contrasts the present era to the repressive military regime which has recently ended. At the same time, it makes the complex point that in this fragile period of political transition, the legacy of the past still haunts people, preventing them from being truly free. Paulina mockingly questions the value of freedom in a society which has only provisionally returned to democracy: "Isn't that what this transition is all about? The Commission can investigate crimes but nobody is punished for them?. . . There's freedom to say anything you want as long as you don't say everything you want?" While political freedom is one major issue in the play, there is also the theme of emotional freedom. "You're still a prisoner," Gerardo tells Paulina, "you stayed behind with them, locked in that basement." Gerardo encourages her to "free yourself from them" in order to put her mind at rest. Paulina, however, is insulted by the implication that her only option is to forget her pain. Yet her solution is no less absolute: she feels she can only put her mind at rest by seeking punishment for her tormentors. In the end, however, she stops short of administering the ultimate punishment of death. It has been speculated that while this action does not liberate her from the pain of her torture and rape, it does grant her freedom from the savagery that afflicted her tormentors.

Justice and Injustice

Death and the Maiden contrasts ideal and practical concepts of justice. Both Paulina and Gerardo perceive the considerable injustices exerted by the former military regime, but they differ in their ideas of how justice can best be served under present circumstances. Gerardo believes in the efficacy of the commission to which he has been appointed, feeling that justice will be served by faithfully investigating human rights abuses and then turning the findings over to the country's courts. Paulina, however, is suspicious of the loyalties of those "same judges who never intervened to save one life in seventeen years of dictatorship." To her mind, justice cannot possibly be served through the channels which presently exist, so she resolutely takes the law into her own hands. The brutality of her past experience is undoubtedly at the root of her position; when Gerardo pleads with her at one point to be "reasonable," she bitterly responds: "You be reasonable. They never did anything to you."

Topics for Further Study

- Summarize the evidence presented that Roberto Miranda is the doctor who raped and tortured Paulina.

Does the play offer convincing evidence for his guilt or innocence?

- Compare director Roman Polanski's film adaptation to Dorfman's original text. Screenwriters Dorfman and Rafael Yglesias altered the play's ending, providing further evidence that Miranda is guilty. Do you think this detracts from the play's original vision?

- How do the life roles or careers of each of the characters seem to be reflected in their actions and beliefs?

- Analyze the different ways the characters view the idea of revenge in the play. In what ways is it presented as satisfying or dissatisfying?

- Research the recent work of human rights tribunals in countries like Chile or Argentina. How do accounts of this process suggest that the individuals involved balance the ethical issues presented in this play?

- Analyze the theatrical device of the mirror which is lowered near the conclusion of the play. What effect(s) does this image achieve?

Memory and Reminiscence

Dorfman commented in an interview with Carlos Reyes on the Amnesty International homepage: "Memory is a constant obsession for me," observing that a memory of the past is a counter against those, like the military rulers, "who would obliterate others, who would forget them, ignore them, neglect them, erase them from the earth." Dorfman's "obsession" shows in his characterization of Paulina, whose strong memories of being raped and tortured still haunt her and provide a challenge to the historical revisionists who would claim that such events did not take place. Establishing a history of the victims will be an important step towards national reconciliation, but the question of just how satisfying such a process can be to Paulina and others like her is one of the more difficult issues presented in the play.

Morality and Ethics

The immorality of the past military regime is not debated in *Death and the Maiden;* the discussion of Paulina's torment and the mention of other cases of extra-judicial abduction, torture, and murder are enough to establish the context. The central ethical issue of the play is whether Paulina, by choosing to try—and punish—Miranda herself, is merely replicating the same injustices of the military regime. "We can't use their methods," Gerardo comments. Paulina agrees in concept but feels that the circumstances are different. She also argues that she is giving Miranda the opportunity to defend himself, a privilege she was not granted.

Style

Death and the Maiden is highly realistic in form and structure, with a plot that rapidly unfolds in linear progression, characters that are fully-realized individuals, and a fixed, recognizable setting. Dorfman breaks with this basic structure only at the end of the play, when the setting jumps to a concert hall several months later. At this point, the playwright introduces an expressionistic device, a mirror aimed at the audience, to bring thematic unity to the piece. A fully realistic play would present some kind of resolution to the dramatic conflict but this is hardly possible in *Death and the Maiden*. Indeed, the play suggests precisely the difficulty of resolving the social issue which is at its heart: how can a society reconcile itself with its violent past and, somehow, move forward?

While it is the tendency of most theater critics to compare the work of different playwrights in order to give their readers a point of reference for a particular work, this has rarely been the case in the published criticism of *Death and the Maiden*. Critics have not been so focused on applying labels to Dorfman's theatrical technique, perhaps because they do not consider Dorfman—an intellectual and academic internationally known for his essays, novels, and poetry—to be primarily a playwright. Additionally, the content and political context of *Death and the Maiden* being so novel to English and American audiences, critics have focused more on these elements than on categorizing Dorfman's dramatic style.

As an exception to this tendency, one playwright with whom Dorfman is often related is Harold Pinter. The British playwright has remained an important touchstone for Dorfman; his first book was an academic study of the politics of oppression in Pinter's early play *The Room*, and he dedicates *Death and the Maiden* to Pinter. The connections between the two writers, however, are related more to their political investments than their dramatic techniques. An article by Stephen Gregory in *Comparative Drama*, for example, suggested how a retrospective reading of Dorfman's study of Pinter illustrates "how it anticipates both the concerns of his later work on Latin America and the issues that will unite the two writers some twenty years after its publication." Dorfman hardly works in the style of Pinter, a playwright associated with the Theatre of the Absurd.

Literally meaning "out of harmony," the term absurd was the existentialist Albert Camus's designation for the situation of modern men and women whose lives lack meaning as they drift in an inhuman universe. *Death and the Maiden* explores a political context which could properly be described as absurd, as a military regime prevents individuals from exerting any control over their own destiny. In terms of theatrical technique, however, Dorfman's play remains realistic in form without the stylistic exaggeration of Pinter's work, or that of other playwrights, such as Samuel Beckett (*Waiting for*

Godot) and Eugene Ionesco (*The Bald Soprano*), who are usually labeled as absurdists.

While *Death and the Maiden* resists comparison with the work of contemporary playwrights, many have observed that it functions something like Greek tragedy. "More than one critic," wrote John Butt in the *Times Literary Supplement*, "has commented on this production's formal perfection, the way it unwinds with a remorseless inevitability that recalls the finest classical tragedy." In form, of course, the play differs from tragedy on many levels: it lacks, for example, the downfall and death of a hero or heroine and the "anagnorisis" or self-recognition on the part of that character about the mistake that led to his or her demise. Still, the parallels exist; Mimi Kramer noted in the *New Yorker* that "the play observes classical rules about unity of time and place, and about offstage violence."

Dorfman himself has used the term tragedy to refer to the work, responding to the suggestion that the play functions as political propaganda by saying in *Index on Censorship* that "tragedies are never propaganda, ever." This comment is merely a suggestion of the thematic and dramatic complexity of the work, but Dorfman has explored the idea of tragedy further by examining the concept of catharsis, the social function of classical tragedy by which audiences would purge themselves of certain emotions. "The play," Dorfman stated in the same article, "is not just a denunciation of how bad torture is. It aims to help purge ourselves of pity and terror." In Greek society, the catharsis of tragedy helped to unify people, and Dorfman implies a hope that his play might serve the same role in Chilean society, further enabling the process of reconciliation with that country's past atrocities.

The device of the mirror at the conclusion of the play contributes most strongly to the process of catharsis. In an interview in the London *Times*, Dorfman said, in reference to the audience, that *Death and the Maiden* "is not a play about somebody else, it's a play about them." The mirror coming down is a device which implicates them in the moral dilemma. "People are going to watch themselves and ask: 'what would I do, who am I in the midst of all this?'" The mirror is also the element which separates the play from its realistic form and structure; it leaves the audience with a powerful image at the conclusion of a play whose central conflict remains otherwise unresolved.

Historical Context

Ariel Dorfman carefully specifies in his stage directions that *Death and the Maiden* is set in "a country that is probably Chile but could be any country that has given itself a democratic government just after a long period of dictatorship." There is both a specificity and a universality to the play, as many critics have noted, making it extremely topical in the late-twentieth century era of tentative political transformation. Frank Rich of the *New York Times*, for example, called the play a "mousetrap designed to catch the conscience of an international audience at a historic moment when many more nations than Chile are moving from totalitarian terror to fragile freedom." John Butt similarly found the play "timely," saying that it catches the audience "in a neat moral trap" by making them "confront choices that most would presumably leave to the inhabitants of remote and less favoured countries."

Among the many Latin American countries which in recent decades have similarly experienced periods of military rule (Guatemala, Brazil, Bolivia), Argentina and Chile are often compared to one another because of their shared history and close geographical proximity in the "Southern Cone" of South America. Both Chile, following Augusto Pinochet's military coup, and Argentina, in the years of the military's "Dirty War," were characterized by civil repression, extra-judicial abductions and "disappearances," torture, and murder. Familiarity with the modern history of these two countries provides a good basis of understanding for the context of *Death and the Maiden*.

Throughout the first half of the twentieth century in Chile, the political climate swung often between right and left with no government strong enough to effect large scale change. Infrastructure developed slowly and rural poverty became an increasing problem, along with rapid urbanization as desperate populations flooded the city. Some social reforms were achieved in the 1960s, but Chile's politics became increasingly polarized and militant. Salvador Allende crept to presidential victory in 1970 with a leftist coalition of socialists, communists, and extremists. Allende's sweeping economic reforms included the state takeover of many private enterprises; the United States was angered by the confiscation of U.S.-controlled copper mines and Chile's openly friendly relationship with Cuba, a country with whom America had ceased diplomatic and economic ties.

The Chilean military, in a coup orchestrated by General Augusto Pinochet, seized power on September 11, 1973, using air force jets to bomb the presidential palace. (U.S. support of the coup through the Central Intelligence Agency [CIA] has been documented.) Allende died, apparently a suicide, and thousands of his supporters were killed. Pinochet, at the head of a four-man ruling junta (a group or council that controls a government), dissolved Chile's congress and repressed—often violently—political opposition. His government maintained power for the next decade and a half, frequently resorting to terror (including the abduction/tortures to which Paulina was subjected) in order to suppress dissent.

Compare & Contrast

- **1992:** Augusto Pinochet, who handed over the Chilean presidency in 1990 to democratically-elected Patricio Aylwin Azocar, remains commander in chief of the army.

  Today: Pinochet has stepped down as army commander but in March, 1998, was bestowed the title of senator for life, despite widespread protest.

- **1992:** With Pinochet still their commander in chief, the Chilean armed forces continue to wield a good deal of autonomous power in Chilean society.

  Today: There is still considerable tension between the government and the military concerning the human rights violations of the Pinochet era. Although current president Eduardo Frei has accelerated human rights tribunals and inquiries into Chile's "disappeared," punishment of the perpetrators remains extremely difficult.

- **1992:** The era of Apartheid is gradually drawing to a close in South Africa, with whites voting two to one in a referendum to give President F. W. de Klerk a mandate to end white-minority rule. A June massacre in a black township, however, and charges of police involvement in the case, suggest the pressing need for more rapid transformation.

  Today: While many political, social, and economic difficulties remain for South Africa, the peaceful transfer of power to President Nelson Mandela makes the country an excellent example of how a society can make the difficult transition to democracy.

- **1992:** Peru's President Alberto Fujimori suspends the Constitution April 5, and assumes dictatorial powers in the fight against corruption and Maoist guerrilla group Sendera Luminosa ("Shining Path"). The United States suspends aid to Peru.

  Today: On April 22, 1997, President Fujimori orders a military attack against a group of leftist guerrillas who have held hostages for several months in the Japanese embassy in the capitol of Lima. All fourteen of the guerrillas are killed, along with two soldiers, and one of the hostages; many others are wounded. Fujimori's actions are celebrated internationally, but nagging issues remain, including damaged relations with Japan (who had pushed for a peaceful negotiation to end the standoff), and accusations that Fujimori has used government intelligence forces to investigate political opponents. Throughout Latin America, the continued existence of guerrilla activity combined with hard-line government policies suggest the continued fragility of many of the region's democracies.

A peaceful transfer of presidential power was achieved in 1990 but considerable tension continued between the military and the government concerning the human rights violations of the Pinochet era. Under a constitution written during his regime, Pinochet himself remained army commander until stepping down in March, 1998. Yet after that time he still retained congressional influence with the title of senator for life. Chilean society continues to struggle with the violent legacy of its past, although current president Eduardo Frei has sped the process of reconciliation by accelerating human rights tribunals and inquiries into Chile's "disappeared" (through commissions like the one to which Gerardo has been appointed in *Death and the Maiden*).

Chile's neighbor, Argentina, has likewise seen frequent suppression of democratic processes. The country experienced its first coup in 1930, the government falling to a coalition of military officers and civilian aristocrats who established a semi-fascist state following the growing trend of fascism in Europe. The military undertook a more forceful coup in 1943, one which set out to restructure Argentine culture totally. The goal this time was not the mere suppression of political radicals but the complete eradication of civilian politics. There were to be five more coups between 1943 and 1976, the year in which the military initiated the brutality known as the Dirty War. During this period, Argentina's most influential ruler was Colonel Juan Peron, first elected to the presidency in 1946.

Peron was different from his military predecessors in that he sought to integrate the urban working class into his party, although his government retained a strong hand on more hard-line radicalism. Peron's partner in everything during the early years of his presidency was his mistress, later his wife, Eva Duarte—known popularly as Evita (composer Andrew Lloyd Weber and lyricist Tim Rice would immortalize her in their 1978 musical *Evita*). She had cunning political instinct, upon which Peron grew to rely. When the military threw Peron over in 1955, many of the social changes he and Evita had initiated remained in place. The legacy of Evita (she died of cancer in 1952), combined with the knowledge that Peron was alive in exile, empowered many to adhere to Peronist ideals, despite the military's attempts to suppress them. Peron was resurrected in 1973 as the economic situation in Argentina continued to worsen, and the public, looking for some positive way out of the military regimes, enthusiastically welcomed his return; he died a mere eight months into his new term as president.

A coup on March 24, 1976, overthrew Peron's widow Isabel, president since his death, and a military junta composed of the three commanders in chief of the armed forces installed itself as the government. In the years between the coup and the resumption of democratic elections in 1983, the military fought a vicious and covert war against the people of Argentina, totally restructuring society to eradicate any political consciousness. A system of clandestine concentration camps, numbering over three hundred at their peak, provided the center of an all-out policy of abduction, torture, murder, and disposal. Estimates of the dead run as high as thirty thousand, and the lives of the survivors were left destroyed in other ways. As in Chile, following a tenuous return to democracy Argentine society at large continues to struggle with the issue of how to rectify the violence of the past. Activists such as Las Madres de Plaza de Mayo (who daringly initiated protests against the military government while it was still in power) maintain pressure on the current government to investigate human rights abuses, although punishment for many of the perpetrators remains unlikely.

Critical Overview

From the time of its debut, the international reception of *Death and the Maiden* was largely positive, extending Dorfman's reputation as an important writer and intellectual. Reviews of the Broadway production were less enthusiastic, but critics differ on whether the weaknesses were the result of failings in the play, the performances (Glenn Close, Richard Dreyfuss, and Gene Hackman), or the direction of Mike Nichols. English and American audiences lacked the political experience of a recent return to democracy, shared by so many emerging nations in this era, yet the play is easily accessible to them. Matt Wolf wrote in the *Times* of London that the play was an unlikely success given its topic, but "Dorfman argues that its time is now. 'It clearly has touched some sort of nerve, some sort of centre.'" As "a play about the empowerment of women," *Death and the Maiden* grounds the anger of Paulina in concrete historical circumstances, yet universalizes it. "Her rage," Dorfman stated to Wolfe, "comes out of something. . . that can be understood as the product of a system. At the same time, she is clearly speaking for more than torture victims."

Also inspired by the excellence of the London production, Andrew Graham-Yooll commented in *Index on Censorship*, "The conflict between the three characters, the suspect's denial, the woman's search for revenge, and the husband's need for justice, create gripping, thrilling and intense theatre." The *Times Literary Supplement's* Butt, meanwhile, called the play "harrowing." He observed that *Death and the Maiden* might draw some criticism for failing to provide any solutions to the moral dilemma it presents, any "easy answers to the question of how the new democracies should deal with the criminals in their midst." The critic, however, found this dramatic choice to be more true to experience and a real strength of the play: "In fact, the play's depressing message is that none of the three characters can offer a solution because all are still reliving the past."

In citing negative aspects of the Broadway production, Frank Rich of the *New York Times* nevertheless praised the strength of Dorfman's play. What makes it "ingenious," he wrote, is the playwright's "ability to raise such complex issues within a thriller that is full of action and nearly devoid of preaching." Rich found that despite the heavy star power of the Broadway production, its light tone diminished the inherent strengths of Dorfman's complex play. Rich wrote that "it is no small feat that the director Mike Nichols has managed to transform 'Death and the Maiden' into a fey domestic comedy. But what kind of feat, exactly?" Rich found the direction and characterizations flat and one-dimensional, producing an ironic and "tedious trivialization of Ariel Dorfman's work." Nichols took a similar approach in his film version of Edward Albee's *Who's Afraid of Virginia Woolf?* noted Rich but there produced a "funnier though still valid alternative" to the play. "But what exactly," wondered Rich about the current production, "is the point of his jokey take on a play whose use of the word death in the title is anything but ironic?"

Mimi Kramer in the *New Yorker* similarly criticized the Broadway production in comparison to the London one but found the inadequacies to be a product of Dorfman's "obvious" and "flaccid" play. "The questions raised by 'Death and the Maiden' have been oft before but ne'er so ploddingly explored," she wrote. The play takes too long to set up its central conflict, Kramer felt, dwells too long on the irony of Paulina contemplating doing just what her tormentors did to her, and "never gets much beyond that idea." Thomas M. Disch of the *Nation* also found that the weaknesses of the play and of the production reflected one another. "The plot is all too simple," he wrote, the characters "generic and hollow," and Dorfman "neither engages one's emotions nor thinks through the situation with any rigor." The director cannot be blamed for the result, Disch concluded, "nor yet can the cast, who do no more and no less than Hollywood stars usually do—play themselves, for lack of any better-defined roles."

In concert with Kramer, John Simon identified weaknesses in Dorfman's play. He wrote in *New York* magazine of the "unconvincing" devices which establish the dramatic situation in the play, and other flaws of technique. "Yet these are small matters," he continues, "compared to the basic insufficiency of reducing a national and individual tragedy to a mere whodunit." For Simon, the play fails because of this trivialization. And whereas Butt found the lack of resolution in the play to be a strength, Simon argued that because the play "avoids coming satisfactorily to grips with the one question it raises," it cannot succeed as a whodunit, either.

Jack Kroll of *Newsweek* also argued that Dorfman lessened the impact of his play by turning it into a "whodunnit." One effect of his choice was that it allowed the director, quoted as saying "God preserve us all from a true political play," to turn the production into a "domestic imbroglio." Kroll's assessment falls somewhere in between Simon, who found the play a failure, and Rich, who argued its strength despite the nature of the Broadway production. *Death and the Maiden* remains "a fiercely political play," Kroll commented, and if Dorfman had only forced his character Miranda to face his own guilt, this one change could have produced the "masterwork" that many critics have called the play, and enabled the star actors "to reach an emotional focus that they only glancingly hit in this production."

Apart from reviews of the premiere productions and interviews with Dorfman, there exists yet little criticism of *Death and the Maiden*. Most articles and other extended works on Dorfman focus on his novels, poetry, or his experience as a critic and artist in exile. One exception is Stephen Gregory's lengthy article for *Comparative Drama*, which explores parallels between Dorfman and

British playwright Harold Pinter.

What Do I Read Next?

- *Widows*, a 1981 novel by Dorfman, later adapted into a play of the same name. *Widows* focuses on a group of thirty-seven women who suspect that their missing husbands have been abducted and killed by authorities of their government. Dorfman set the novel in occupied Greece in the 1940s to avoid censorship but changed the setting to Chile when he created the stage adaptation. Depicting the experience of people seeking justice under a repressive regime, *Widows* provides an interesting counterpoint to *Death and the Maiden*.

- *How to Read Donald Duck:*

Imperialist Ideology in the Disney Comic, an early work of criticism by Dorfman, which illustrates his argument that forms of popular literature such as comic books have historically been used to promote capitalist ideology and encourage passivity, specifically for the benefit of American business interests in Latin America.

- *La casa de los espiritus* (1982), the first novel by Isabel Allende, now one of the world's most widely read Hispanic writers, whose father was first cousin to Chilean President Salvador Allende (the novel was translated by Magda Bogin as *The House of the Spirits* and published by Knopf, 1985). Allende, like Paulina in *Death and the Maiden* helped transport people to avoid military repression after Pinochet's coup. The events she witnessed, "the dead, the tortured, the widows and orphans, left an unforgettable impression on my memory," and were incorporated into this work.

- *Allende: A Novel*, by Fernando Alegria, is a biography of Salvador Allende cast in a novel form, illustrating "how fiction and history occasionally "collide, then merge, enriching and refining each other."

- *Chilean Writers in Exile: Eight Short Novels*, edited by Fernando Alegria (Crossing Press, 1981) presents "an expression of a group of writers who, in spite of all the hardships of life in exile, are producing vigorous statements on behalf of the Chilean people." The collection, which contains Dorfman's *Putamadre*, offers the opportunity to compare different perspectives on Chilean politics and life in exile, as expressed in fiction.

- *Extremities*, by William Mastrosimone, a contemporary American play about a woman victimized by a rapist in her own home, who manages to turn the tables and trap her attacker. The play (which was made into a film in 1986 starring Farah Fawcett) makes an interesting contrast to *Death and the Maiden* because of the revenge theme and the different ways in which it is played out.

Sources

Butt, John. "Guilty Conscience?" in the *Times Literary Supplement*, February 28, 1992, p. 22.

Disch, Thomas M. Review of *Death and the Maiden* in the *Nation*, May 11, 1992, pp. 640-43.

Dorfman, Ariel. Afterword to *Death and the Maiden*, Penguin (New York), 1992, pp. 71-75.

Kramer, Mimi. "Magical Opportunism" in the *New Yorker*, March 30, 1992, p. 69.

Kroll, Jack. "Broadway Mind-Stretchers" in *Newsweek*, March 30, 1992, p. 65.

Reyes, Carlos, and Maggie Patterson. "Ariel Dorfman on Memory and Truth" on the Amnesty International Home Page, http://www.oneworld.org/textver/amnesty/journal_ju

Rich, Frank. "Close, Hackman and Dreyfuss in 'Death and the Maiden'" in the *New York Times*, March 18, 1992, p.C15.

Simon, John. "The Guary Apes" in *New York*, March 30, 1992, pp. 87-88.

Wolf, Matt. "Power Games at Home" in the *Times* (London), November 4, 1991, p. 14.

Further Reading

Contemporary Literary Criticism, Gale: Vol. 48, 1988, Vol. 77, 1993.

> This resource compiles selections of criticism; it is an excellent starting point for a research paper on Dorfman. The selections in these two volumes span Dorfman's career up to 1993 (criticism of *Death and the Maiden* is found in Volume 77). Dorfman is also covered in *Hispanic Writers, Hispanic Literary Criticism*, and Volume 130 of *Contemporary Authors*.

Graham-Yooll, Andrew. "Dorfman: A Case of Conscience" in *Index on Censorship*, Vol. 20, no. 6, 1991, pp. 3-4.

> An interview with Dorfman in which the playwright discusses Chile's transition to democracy and his own plays *Reader* and *Death and Maiden*.

Gregory, Stephen. "Ariel Dorfman and Harold Pinter: Politics of the Periphery and Theater of the Metropolis" in *Comparative Drama*, Vol. 30, no. 3, 1996, pp. 325-45.

> An article that fleshes out the "string of contingencies" between these two writers. Gregory's article presents "a

summary of the writers' respective political involvements and commitments," continues with an analysis of several plays (including *Death and the Maiden*), and concludes "with a retrospective political reading of Dorfman's study of Pinter to show how it anticipates both the concerns of his later work on Latin America and the issues that will unite the two writers some twenty years after its publication."

Guzman, Patricio. *The Battle of Chile* (re-release), First Run/Icarus Films, 1998.

A documentary, produced in the years 1973-1976, which is still banned in Chile to this day. The film presents a leftist perspective on Salvador Allende's presidency, the coup of Pinochet, and the first "years of terror" following the installation of the dictatorship. Guzman's more recent work also includes the film *Chile: The Persistent Memory*.

Skidmore, Thomas E. and Peter H. Smith. *Modern Latin America*, fourth edition, Oxford University Press (New York), 1997.

A comprehensive, general resource on the interrelated political histories of this vast region. It is particularly useful in understanding the context of Dorfman's play, applicable to Chile as well as to a number of other Latin American countries who have experienced periods of military repression. Students interested specifically in the history of modern Chile may investigate some of the many books on the topic, such as Mark Falcoff's *Modern Chile, 1970-1989: A Critical History* (published by Transaction, 1989).

Lightning Source UK Ltd.
Milton Keynes UK
UKHW020741140922
408851UK00009B/886